10 Secrets to

Networking

Success

by

PAUL EDWARDS

10 Secrets to Networking Success

How to Build a Network of Super Affiliates to Promote and Endorse Your Brand in Only 90 Days

PAUL EDWARDS

First Edition.

ISBN 9781732314405
LCCN 2018943351

Printed by Village Books in Bellingham, WA

v061818

Table of Contents

PREFACE

For several years prior to writing, I worked in Olympia, Washington as an insurance salesman.

It was, for me, a season that began in disappointment. I answer to the calling of "Communicator," and fully intended to begin a career in radio and broadcasting after completing my degree and leaving military service. Instead, I found myself learning the practice of selling insurance policies as a necessity, to pay bills and remain gainfully employed.

By the time this excursion commenced, insurance salesmen were a long-maligned and lampooned caricature. My generation grew up laughing at the farcical portrayal by Stephen Tobolowsky of Ned Ryerson in *Groundhog Day*, and the proliferation of Internet commerce had reduced the product to a "race to the bottom" commodity.

In transition from my first job with American Family Insurance to Liberty Mutual Insurance, however, I received an unexpected word from my new branch manager.

"You should not be in this office all day," he told me during interviews. "A big part of the way we do things is by getting *out* of the office and being visible in the community."

I barely understood what he meant at the time, but heeding his advice began a journey that led me to writing this book.

In September of 2013, fresh on the trail of building my book of business at Liberty, I went to my very first networking event - the Thurston County Multiple Listings Sales Association's (MLSA) weekly breakfast meeting and tour. I didn't really know what to do while I was there, but I knew enough to know that if I was going to get any business out of networking, I'd have to attend consistently.

Leading off with MLSA, I started to show up at meetings, events, and networking opportunities all over town. I didn't realize, until I got recruited away from Liberty two years later, how much I would become "The Face" of an office that averaged about seven to nine sales reps. Most of my colleagues at Liberty did far less networking than I did, if any. It wouldn't be a stretch to assume that many people thought I was the local Liberty agent, if they didn't know better or already work with one of my colleagues.

In the spring of 2015, when I left Liberty for Insurance Services Group, I had such momentum from all of the networking that I was able to promise my new leadership, "I will be binding business on Day One when I begin working with you." It was no exaggeration, and it wasn't merely my own personal insurance policies. I had people lined up waiting to sign.

Some time after that, I got nominated to lead a networking group with the Lacey Chamber of Commerce. One day, while leading the meeting, my good friend and future business coach Alan Shimamoto suggested I create a seminar-style presentation about networking itself, as a means of making the meetings more valuable and interesting to the attendees.

So, in a twist of fate, I created the presentation known as "Networking Intentionally," which ended up inspiring Alan in reverse. He went on to launch the "IN Team," his entrepreneurial networking group. The words "IN TEAM" form the acronym for "Intentionally Networking Together, Everyone Achieves More."

Another two years passed before it dawned on me that I was rehearsing and presenting the initial substance of my new career, the one I was truly created to have. With each repetition of the presentation, I further cemented myself as someone who gave an informative, valuable and educational talk.

10 Secrets to Networking Success is, largely, one man's guide to becoming "The Face" of your business wherever you ply your trade. We exist in an age where the demand for strategy and knowledge is greater than ever. With the old guard in full retreat, certainty ahead of the curve is the currency of Generation X and Millennials. It's my observation that the more you can present yourself as someone willing to cater to that demand, the more success you will enjoy in return. This holds especially true if you market a product or service like insurance.

Even if your product has a lot of flash to it, networking groups aren't storefronts. You're going to need something more interesting to talk about once a group is accustomed to your presence. Why wouldn't we position ourselves as valuable to our community in more than one category? I could have made this book solely about networking; I have enough experiences and stories to tell from that category alone, but I know enough about Communication - written, spoken or simply displayed - to multiply value to you.

Let's begin, however, with networking. That's where it started for me. If you haven't made use of it yet, or you're wondering how to do it effectively, the rest will come in time.

Part One

Face To Face

CHAPTER ONE

NETWORKING INTENTIONALLY

Much of my career, after leaving the military and graduating college, relied on the strength of many rather than the strength of one.

I got my first insurance job by going for an informational interview and allowing my employer to "test-drive" how he felt about hiring me; my second came on referral recommendation from an affiliate within the company; my third from being recruited over LinkedIn.

I decided to write this book because of the settled confidence I have in meeting people, forming relationships with them, and exchanging ways of benefiting each other. I knew I had a massive network of people I could turn to for help, advice and resources. I knew that wherever I went in the future, that network would only expand.

During those first several months, however, I bumbled as much as anyone. I was salesy, far too eager to talk about insurance and didn't really understand how to handle fellow networkers with rhythm and grace. Sometimes I would just be flat-out aggressive, asking people who they currently used for their insurance just minutes after meeting them.

On the upside, however, I'm not one to be blind to the writing on the wall. When people began to distance themselves from me, I made no assumption that it was personal. I took a look at my own behavior and figured they had good reason to do so; I was ravenous to sell, as we all are in the early, lean years of business. There wasn't a huge pre-existing source of income paying my bills. I needed to get policies on the books, and fast.

As a bonus, I was unafraid to test any networking opportunity I could credibly attend. I spent 80% of my time in 2013-2015 out of the office, going as far north from Olympia as Seattle and Bellevue and as far south as Vancouver and Portland, to try and cultivate contacts.

Much of my long-distance efforts in networking were, it turned out, wastes of time and money. Geographical limitations still play a part in things, no matter how amiable you are in the eyes of the people you meet. For all of the time I spent in Seattle, for example, I made <u>one</u> contact who got as far as buying from me. The rest were mere pleasantries and "Nice to meet you, nice knowing you."

In the bigger picture, these mistakes gave <u>me</u> all the insight I needed. By reading and applying what I've experienced and written, <u>you</u> don't need to make the same errors. By getting a clear, concise picture of what you're actually doing when you go to a networking function, you can be 100% genuine and never have to overcome the perception of being salesy. And by committing yourself to principles and practices that fulfill and uphold the *purpose* of networking, you can be the best of both worlds - you can be enriched while enriching others.

So let's get started, discuss in-depth the principles I use, and start building your brand personality.

CHAPTER TWO

CONSISTENCY

Either show up consistently to a networking group, or you may as well not exist, in the minds of those present.

People who show up to once and never come back are correct either way - it was a waste of their time. If they don't return because they *know* they don't want to return, they've wasted time well; if they don't return because they just can't be bothered, they've wasted time poorly.

In the radio advertising business, my good friend Bobby Jackson emphasized that: "Radio is 'what you say' times 'how many times you say it.'" In-person networking is very much like a TV or radio ad. We don't know the slogans "Fifteen minutes could save you 15 percent" or "What's in your wallet?" because GEICO and Capital One run their commercials once or twice a year. You shouldn't expect to be well-known for doing any less.

My good friend Richard Bokofsky, an independent life insurance broker, became notorious in several groups in Olympia because he always ended whatever he said with the same slogan: "You don't buy life insurance because you're going to die. You buy life insurance become someone you love is going to live." It got so familiar that it became tradition to chant the slogan along with him as he said it.

Another less-discussed facet of consistency in networking also runs parallel to TV or radio advertising -- legitimacy.

Have you noticed the credibility people ascribe to products and services that are heavily advertised, versus ones that are not? I could persuade insurance customers to buy Liberty Mutual products all day long, but when I wrote surplus lines policies through companies like Colony Specialty and Mesa Underwriters Specialty Insurance Company, they hadn't a clue who I was talking about.

It's the same for you in your network. Show up often, or don't bother. Your frequent or constant presence establishes legitimacy and commitment in their minds, whereas your flightiness does the opposite.

So show up early, and show up often. The network needs repetitive and thorough cultivation; you can't expect it to grow in your absence. I commit to networking groups and make them "standing orders" on my calendar. Start with local business groups, such as the Chamber of Commerce, LeTip, or civic groups like Rotary and Kiwanis. In the absence of knowing people when I started at Liberty Mutual, I simply "showed up" at local groups and introduced myself. I confessed to not knowing anyone and simply wanted to "check things out" and see if they were the right fit.

I like to show up early, in order to have good conversations before the volume of 30 different people having 15 different conversations forces you to speak in raised tones. An odd by-product of intensive networking is that I am now a lover of silence and solitude. I've had so many conversations with so many people for so many days of my life that it's more challenging now to provide value with my presence. I don't like showing up to networking with nothing to add or with my hands out asking for referrals. It has ten times the impact if you see someone at a group and you can pull them aside to say, "I've been trying to get in touch with you, because I found someone who might be able to help you with that problem you mentioned last week."

You are, of course, free to doubt me on this, but the confirmation of the significance of a consistent and devoted member came home to me in the summer of 2015. To comply with my non-compete agreement as I left Liberty, I departed for a time from the Thurston County Chamber Top Flight Leads group. At the time, it was the largest and most attractive group in all of Thurston County with 50 members strong every week. Leaving was the last thing I wanted to do, and after my Liberty replacement dropped out three months later, they quickly brought me back in. I received a round of applause on the first day back in the saddle, after all kinds of heartfelt compliments and remarks of "we miss seeing you at Top Flight" in the interim.

CHAPTER THREE

CARNEGIE IS CRITICAL

My father kept a copy of *How to Win Friends and Influence People* in his personal library as I grew up. I remember discovering and reading it for the first time as a teenager. I was fascinated with its insight into our condition.

This quote from the author, Dale Carnegie, always stuck with me: "We are interested in others when they are interested in us."

There is a drift away from traditional, old-school wisdom on marketing and promoting yourself or your business, a rejection of some of Carnegie's methods in the blurring speed of change in the 21st Century. I couldn't agree more with getting rid of outdated selling methods, but what we're talking about here is an observation of the human condition that does not change.

Over time, I learned that focusing on the needs of others does not have an off-season. Whether I am flush with new business and struggling to keep up with it all, or in a slump and needing some good news, the best thing I maintained was an interest in my associates and community's well-being. It is important to do this with a sincere heart, not expecting anything in return. (You will get things in return, but do not *expect* them as a condition of doing what you do).

For many years, I've believed this to be true. I haven't always felt comfortable about its practicality, because not everyone responds to outward, others-oriented gestures the same way. Were I to be given permission to qualify Mr. Carnegie's statement, I would add to it the wisdom of Christ: "Do not … cast your pearls before swine…" (Matthew 7:6, NKJV).

Doing networking to the level I've done it meant plenty of disappointment from non-responsive people who can't be bothered to return the sentiment. If you walk into a meeting with a pure sales agenda, it won't be long before you lose heart. Fellow members are a thousand times more interested in growing *their* business and making *their* sales than they are in yours.

Another elephant in the room we should name is what I call "obvious referral partners." This is because some industries rely heavily on networking as a means of acquiring business, while others are not. Attorneys, for example, are notoriously difficult to pin down into a standard group, as are trade contractors and highly-skilled professionals like doctors and dentists. It's not been my experience that they even send their staff marketing officers on a consistent basis to networking events.

However, I've never been to a group where multi-level marketers, insurance salesmen, Edward Jones advisors, mortgage brokers and life/business coaches weren't present. Depending on what you do, you may find yourself an "obvious" referral partner.

Obvious referral sources are likely connected with several other people vying with you to get their referral business. For this reason, when I sold insurance, I made a point of keeping quiet about business when talking with loan officers and financial advisors unless they brought it up. I kept conversations fun, casual, conversational, and focused on their lives and their interests. I didn't talk "business" until it was time to do business.

In short, the only thing "obvious" about these relationships is that you need to pay attention to the obvious: if you charge straight at them asking for referrals, you're liable to end up blacklisted.

People you meet aren't *automatically* interested in buying your product just because they show interest in it. This ought to go without saying; we know in personal relationships that politeness doesn't equal interest in being friends … why assume otherwise in business?

I have made assumptions, and had them made about me, by people desperate to make a sale, that conversational interest about a product or service translates into the desire to buy it. They're the kind of advances I'm glad are not caught on video somewhere, because I wince to think of them, especially when I was the one making the assumption.

CHAPTER FOUR

RELATIONSHIPS WITH LIFT

Be Engaged

I've always been surprised by people who think you go to a networking event to make sales "on the spot." That's absurd. It's like going to church on Sunday, thinking that the people there will act as your intimate allies simply because you go to the same church service.

Subtler still, I have walked into networking meetings where I've been introduced as an insurance broker and had people tell me on the spot, "You and I need to talk. I have some issues regarding my insurance and need some answers." They passed me their business card, we chatted for several minutes, and then I followed up with a phone call or e-mail only to never hear from them again.

I had this strange idea that I could succeed mainly with shallow, surface-based relationships. I didn't understand what people actually meant when they approached me. I mean, if people tell you to your face, "I want to talk to you about my insurance," I tend to take that as a fairly positive sign they're at least open to doing business with me.

Well, perhaps on the East Coast. In western Washington, it can be a very peculiar way of saying "I'd like to meet for coffee and get to know you." It seems easier to me to say, "I'd like to meet for coffee and get to know you," but I've had no luck changing it.

By contrast, the practical effects of inviting someone out to lunch or coffee, and spending time learning about them personally and professionally, have paid me lengthy dividends. Though it would be inappropriate to presume, the results speak for themselves – when you place a premium on the success and time of people you meet, they end up becoming your best unpaid sales force. I have several clients who, for the price of an occasional three-dollar cup of coffee at Starbucks, made me their primary referral source for insurance needs, and then ended up sending their clients and friends to me as well.

The way into the depths of a business relationship is the "one-on-one." It eliminates the noise of the networking group and creates your first "learning opportunity" about the other person. I use the term "opportunity" because I want you to see, as I do, a faint trace of dollar signs with the things people tell you about themselves.

That is, of course, assuming that you hold the one-on-one meeting to learn about *them*, and not talk much about *yourself*.

You don't schedule a one-on-one to sell people. It's to <u>find out who THEY are, and how you can help THEM</u>. Each person you meet in a network setting is a potential asset to you, but they are a human being first and foremost. Human beings operate according to certain laws, including this old forgotten one: "You scratch my back, and I'll scratch yours."

Suppose you don't know where that person is "itching" … you can't scratch their back! So the first thing I do when meeting someone for a one-on-one is to learn *about* them – hobbies, interests, cultural experiences, marriage/children, and so forth. People will talk about themselves all day, and if you're paying attention to what they say, they will tell you extremely valuable information. I say "valuable" in the sense that *you can add value to it,* but not necessarily *get* value out of it.

Don't panic - you *will* get value out of it, just not necessarily where you *think* you will.

Listen to what the other person says to find out *first* how you can be an asset to *them*. What do people who network need? More often than not, they need *more* places to network! You can invite them to other opportunities to meet people. They will often reveal what associations, non-profits, or civic/youth activities they're involved with. They may also mention *difficulties* they're having – meeting someone, getting a reliable service, finding the best deal on a product. If you practice this principle with everyone you meet, over time you'll have no hesitation in providing solutions for them. "Oh, I know a guy who does that …"

Because I met so many people and took so much time to learn about what they were up to, I found people calling me a "mover and a shaker," or describing my activities on their behalf as "pulling rank," as though I were a high-ranking city politician.

This is actually not a bad analogy, nor is it one I adamantly reject. I have very good relationships with people in local politics, but holding public office is about the furthest thing from my mind. You'll gain a lot of mileage, however, by people associating you with *making things happen*, and the way this starts is by being a resource to them.

In the Olympia/Lacey/Tumwater area of Washington, there are three Chambers of Commerce and plenty of other networking groups within certain industries. My good friend Alan Shimamoto, one of my most vital networking partners, even started his entire independent group, the IN Team, based on the local appetite for introductions and business through relationships. Civic organizations like Rotary, Kiwanis, and the Elks Lodge gather regularly. Go to enough of these meetings, especially in your early and lean years, and you'll have no shortage of alternatives to offer someone looking to get their name recognized.

In a later chapter I will share stories about how I've leveraged people's involvement with non-profits, associations, and youth activities to add value to their lives, but suffice it to say that this is another goldmine. Most people in business are likely to lend their support in some capacity to one organization or another, which gives them a very common and predictable set of needs - volunteers and money, mainly, but also materials and supplies.

If you are in the position to help someone procure items for an auction or raffle, I can't tell you what a difference it will make in setting you apart from your competitors in a crowded field. Moreover, if you can assist in alleviating the eternal burden of a shortage of volunteers or money, you will see the rewards come back to you in spades.

Don't tune out when you hear people begin to discuss difficulties they're having. This is your opportunity to become a relational physician, administering care in places where people are freely telling you they're in pain.

The morning I wrote this, a friend popped up my Facebook feed asking for recommendations for a plumber. I was able to recommend two plumbing companies I know, but the best part is that this particular friend was already a huge beneficiary of my recommendations. He is a painter and, by introducing him to some friends of mine in real estate, he's earned a huge extra pile of cash and paid his way out of debt ahead of schedule.

I'm convinced beyond all doubt that I get paid for this, when referral business and opportunities fall out of the sky, unsolicited, from completely unrelated people and places where I have not been prospecting or trying to sell. I could just be sitting at my desk, minding my own business, and the phone rings. While reviewing the edits for this paragraph, for example, a specialty contractor referred by a friend from a Friday lunch called me to request quotes. And all I did beforehand was take one of my competitors to lunch!

Be Everywhere

When you meet people and exchange business cards, they give you plenty of information that isn't printed on them.

Chances are that the person whose business card you just threw away is on Facebook, LinkedIn, InstaGram, or some combination of them. If they're at all active on these convenient social media outlets, they will leave you an open trail of unsolicited pictures, posts, and videos to like and comment on. I set aside 20-30 minutes a day to surf the news feeds, commenting (positively) on what they're up to. This will trigger social media to increase my visibility when they next check *their* news feeds.

Once you've established this link, it's up to you to brand yourself in good taste, by "sharing yourself" – your sense of humor, your achievements, your family, an occasional opinion, a talent you have. It's never been cheaper or easier to brand yourself to the very people with whom you want to do business on the most addictive and frequented media platforms in history.

A friend of mine once demanded to know how I was able to be part of 10 networking groups every week. I laughed as she finished asking me the question, because I wondered who had told her that I was in so many since I belonged to only two distinct groups at the time.

It turned out that she'd been trying out different networking groups, and at every single one she attended, my name came up. In each of those settings, each person who heard a reference to me came up to her and said, "Oh yes, Paul Edwards, he's a part of our group" even when I wasn't really a member.

Facebook made this apparent connection possible. I didn't have to leave my office; people were so accustomed to seeing me either in cyberspace, at local events, or in networking groups that they blurred the distinctions of exactly where and how they encountered me. I once even pushed the boundaries of this by both marveling at and mocking it when I posted on Facebook, "No matter where you go … there I am."

CHAPTER FIVE

NOT-FOR-PROFIT IS FOR-PROFIT

Being Involved

The first time I tried involvement with non-profits was the summer of 2014. I was under nomination for my first office within the local subchapter of the Association of the U.S. Army, with whom I've been active for nearly five years now.

We organized a charity run to benefit the soldiers of the 17th Field Artillery Brigade on Joint Base Lewis-McChord. The event took careful planning and coordinated effort, but I supported it by being an event sponsor, paying $300 to set up a table and pass out trail mix refreshments to tired runners.

It was from this event that I began to make a habit of showing up in some fashion at events related to charitable causes. I got invited to auctions, golf tournaments, fall festivals and Christmas parties. Routinely, I'd donate a small amount - $25 to $50 - or help procure an item. My reputation as a fundraising expert soon evolved, and I became known as someone who could draw generosity out of people.

The following year, I was standing in a circle of people at the Lewis County Business Showcase in Chehalis, Washington. The topic was public speaking, and of perhaps 10 people taking turns sharing their feelings on the subject, I was the only one to say, "I love public speaking."

Melinda Wilkes, who owns a janitorial business and was one of the main organizers of the event, stood next to me. She immediately grabbed me by the arm and said, "Good, I'm glad you like public speaking, because you can finish doing the raffle prizes for me." Within moments, I was in my element, standing on the stage and raffling off prizes in my radio announcer voice. I suddenly had ten times the number of eyes and ears on me as I'd had twenty minutes earlier, and people had the opportunity to see the oddball insurance salesman from Thurston County.

Three weeks later, Melinda sent me a note asking if I'd be open to the idea of being the emcee of the Miss Lewis County Pageant. I had no clue about anything related to the

Miss America program, but without hesitation I accepted. I knew enough in the moment to know that my willingness to provide for one of Melinda's needs had led to me providing for another; and I also knew, subconsciously, that providing this need would lead to more networking opportunities.

Accepting Melinda's offer led to me become the male face of the Miss Lewis County pageant - at least so far as hosting duties are concerned - for the last four years. It's a role I relish - I get dressed up like James Bond in a fancy tuxedo and have my photograph taken while surrounded by beautiful young women in evening gowns. Did I mention being an emcee led me to acquiring the largest-premium insurance client I'd ever had? It turned out my co-hostess had a small empire and no agent to help manage its protection.

People's charitable and community causes are actually *inroads* for you to deepen relationships with them. You can donate money, time, labor, or acquire resources on their behalf to simplify the ever-present difficulty of volunteer organizations. It sets you apart in the eyes of your friend who sits on the board or serves as a volunteer.

Two Birds With One Stone

The other way I've seen non-profit involvement work is to donate the products or services of another person in the group to the cause of the person you're trying to make ties with. Pay for Networker A's services and then donate them to the non-profit where Networker B sits on the board.

I figured this out rather easily, because people kept asking me for donations, and you can't donate an insurance policy. I wasn't about to do a cheesy marketing gimmick of donating a "free insurance review." <u>All</u> insurance reviews are free, and everyone knows that.

However, I did notice I had certain clients and friends with businesses who operated through the same networks and personal relationships that I did, *and* had products or services you *could* donate.

For some time now, when solicited for donations, I've alternated between two of my favorite clients in the massage therapy business - Jessie Nearing and Don Harkcom. I purchased 30- or 60-minute massage sessions from them, and then donated them to the foundations, associations or non-profits where other clients or contacts serve as board members or volunteers.

My sons attended Evergreen Christian School, an upscale private school on the west side of Olympia, for a few years. I had a good relationship with Talia Hastie, their marketing director, and learned in 2014 that she was trying to procure items for their spring Visions Auction. When I inquired as to the specifics of what she was looking for, she said, "Oh, I welcome something different or unusual. What do you have in mind?"

Her question gave me a green light to open a door for some friends of mine who were working for Dell's Military Program. Although the program was aimed primarily at procuring government contracts, they also had a division assigned to marketing to the local business community. I scheduled a meeting between Talia and Jessica Lugo, who represented Dell at a networking group we both attended.

Dell ended up donating the tablet we procured for the auction, which was a minor relief for my personal pocketbook. The meeting with Talia went so well that Dell got invited to bid on a deal to replace a substantial portion of the school's aging technology, which ended up saving the school at least $10,000 in projected expenses.

No, I did not get to insure the school or Dell from the deal, because the principle is always the same: the gift horse that comes to you isn't the one you expect. That doesn't mean, though, that your reward is any less tied to your outbound marketing efforts to benefit your fellow man.

In every slow season I've ever had, the way back into momentum has never precluded hard work in service of others' benefit. If your phone isn't ringing and your numbers aren't where they need to be, get out of the office. Reconnect with your friends in marketing and networking, and find out what community projects they're working on. Get on the phone to your network and make things happen for them, and watch as God returns the favor and makes things work for you.

CHAPTER SIX

BE A MAGNET, NOT A PUSHER

Creating Pull

We've all heard the advice, "Don't be salesy in networking groups." No kidding. Everyone knows that, but what do you replace it with? This is not Starbucks; you can't just sit off to the side by yourself and ignore everyone.

"Pushers" are just what they sound like, if you've ever heard the term applied to drug dealers or loan sharks. I've found that even if you're consciously avoiding it, you still can feel pressure to try and *force* things to happen. I used to do this by jumping to the finish line when people would tell me about themselves: "Oh, you need this kind of insurance for that," or "You'd be a great candidate for our single premium whole life product." What rotten cheese!

I've known a few pushers in my time. They can be, outside of their work, very sincere and kind people. Pushing, though, is a phony way to conduct oneself, and I find it extremely ineffective. People see right through the insincerity of pushing.

The difference between a peddler/pusher and a skilled networker is that skilled networkers create a gravitational "pull" that draws people toward them. As an insurance salesman, I had one of the most stereotypically "salesy" occupations in the world, but I created a "pull." Most of my network regards me as anything but "just another salesman."

One of the best ways I do this is staying "ahead of the curve," by which I mean that you present yourself as extremely well read and forward thinking. Because I spend hours listening to podcasts, reading books and attending seminars, my network expects leadership from me. Perhaps best of all, they expect *influential* leadership rather than *positional* leadership. They don't want me to take over their businesses. They simply welcome and respond enthusiastically when I provide ideas, quotes and examples that they can understand and use.

Another way I can describe the process of creating "pull" comes from the catchphrase "create a culture" -- to stand out as a positional leader, or a beacon or symbol. There are many different ways to do it. In some groups, I took leadership positions, such as the board or presidency. Elsewhere, I created events and groups *outside* of the networking format to give members opportunities they otherwise wouldn't have. As I'm fond of saying, I believe in "happening" to your network; you don't just show up, but you bring the presence of someone who imparts value to the people around you.

Smoke 'Em If Ya Got 'Em

I've developed notoriety in Olympia as the chief source of energy behind the monthly game of Texas Hold 'Em at Cigar Daddies, a local boutique smoke shop with a private club. I absolutely love the place; it's a throwback to the speakeasies and smoke-filled boardrooms of our grandfathers' business generation. My good friend Chance Wehrer owns it, and he's made it a haven for the middle-class masculine soul.

In the spring of 2014, I scheduled a meeting with Wes Martin, who owns Sound Business Brokers in downtown Olympia. We'd become friends on Facebook, but not yet met in person, so I made overtures via Instant Messenger and we met at his office. During the back-and-forth, Wes mentioned that he missed having a monthly poker game with his employees, a tradition at an HVAC company he'd previously owned.

Almost immediately, I had the vision in my head of bringing together a bunch of businessmen to play cards and smoke cigars. I had already been over to Cigar Daddies a few times, just to look the place over, and noticed that they had poker tables in the lounge. So Wes and I excitedly discussed the idea of inviting a bunch of people to play poker and enjoy stogies.

I started primitively, using e-mail to invite everyone. At our first game, we had four players, and at the second one only three showed up, but I kept at it, and the game grew. We added Terry Toth, one of my closest friends and a lively, animated real estate broker. He brought a lot of energy and humor into the experience. The intersection of all of these personalities made our games interesting, and the rest of the world began to notice as I kept snapping photos and uploading them to Facebook.

Soon even my competitors asked to join our poker games. The funny thing was that the people watching on Facebook saw this as a very private and exclusive event, but

I had wanted from the beginning to get new faces there every month.

Two years later, with a regular attendance of 16-20 players every month, I floated the idea to the board of the Association of the US Army about putting the game on steroids. We arranged with the Lucky Eagle Casino to have a private room with appetizers and professional dealers running the games. Everyone had to buy in for at least $100 to benefit the soldiers and families we supported. Now past its second year, the game is becoming a fixture in the landscape of the Olympia/Lacey/Tumwater business community, not to mention all of the business that's been done over that poker table.

We do not promote ourselves as a networking group, nor will we ever do so, but $20 to buy into a friendly game of cards and enjoy fine cigars and a man cave for the evening is a big draw, one that keeps the men coming back month after month. It hasn't been just business for me, but the men have traded with each other as well. Real estate deals, funeral arrangements, mortgages, auto detailing, land development, landscaping, HVAC work, and pest inspections get arranged during these games. These relationships became investments that provided returns in plentiful supply, even while sitting in my office and minding my own business.

CHAPTER SEVEN

TEACH APPLICATION, NOT JUST INFORMATION

It's the 21st Century. We're besieged by information, data, statistics, and facts, 24 hours a day, seven days a week. We don't need more information; we need someone to help us understand *what to do* with the information we have.

For as many people who tell you how they avoided disaster through wisdom, there are also stars of achievement that created new markets by ignoring it. The insurance industry's so-called wisdom on marketing was a constant source of frustration to me, with legal nannies and political correctness gone wild. It is not only important to *know* the facts, but to also *understand* the truth.

My good friend Tiana Kleinhoff, a property manager, freely gives out her knowledge and information about her business, stating that "Information is always free." I am glad of it, because property management sounds about as exciting to me as insurance probably does to her. Or you.

After I heard her use this phrase on occasion, I suggested a modification - "Information is always free, but *application* costs money."

I can't speak for Tiana, but I exist in an industry where, in a strange twist on the saying that "The customer is always right," I also have to deal with the mantra that "The professional is always wrong." This simply means that I fight an uphill battle in a marketplace where many potential clients are too clever by half, assuming that what they read online or heard from Aunt Selma, who knows about these things, must automatically be true.

Because I'm presumed lacking in knowledge or accuracy, my knowledge and products are cheapened. Insurance is a commodity in this day and age, particularly with the Internet killing off the profitability of salespeople. I frequently found myself on the receiving end of business I earned at the eleventh hour, when my options were fewest, my earnings minimal, and the client's coverages are mediocre while their prices are high.

Perhaps the insurance business doesn't lend itself to this truth, but in the business of educating and inspiring people, that's a different ball of wax. Suffice it to say you can find yourself in my shoes no matter what industry you're in. Often, people whose levels of access to free information outweighs their ability to interpret it need a skilled guide like you.

When teaching, I avoid industry jargon and "inside baseball" lingo … or if I must use it, I preface it by declaring it to be so. Industry language is fine if you're talking to an audience of peers or competitors in your specific industry, but I constantly remind myself to speak in a language my audience can understand. If you are speaking or writing to people about a specific concept or object, and you aren't certain of their degree of familiarity, *go to the trouble of explaining it.* Speak concisely enough that you don't lose the interest or attention of the rest of the audience who already have a working knowledge of what you're discussing.

I also avoid content that people don't care about or won't find useful. The average audience of marketers, business owners, and networkers would much rather hear about how to multiply revenue using social media than deductibles and escape clauses. Insurance gave me a wonderful lead-in to this since it's a subject everyone prefers not to discuss. As a joke, I would invoke the famous line from the movie *Fight Club*: "The first rule of Selling Insurance is … you do *not talk* about Selling Insurance."

The other thing I do is teach "the how" of applying information by using stories and examples from my own life, particularly those of failure and error. I try to tell people "Here's how to do it" without using the words "Here's how to do it," because the words set different expectations for different people. You may have noticed that much of my writing in this book is based on stories of me screwing things up, or going about them the wrong way before I learned how to do them the right way. In seminars, I will often ask, "Would you like to hear about how I went about things the wrong way?" to put the negative side of the story out in the open for people to examine.

By using the approach of highlighting your own failures, you help people understand their mistakes and failures and see where they're going wrong without pointing fingers. If you're lucky, you catch them *before* they make the mistake, and they're even more grateful.

PART TWO

IN PRINT

CHAPTER EIGHT

WRITING TO GET A RESPONSE

Target the Need

If there's one thing most people hate, it's being ignored or dismissed.

It might be better than being beaten to a pulp, but still better is to know that your words and intentions matter, and they are received and considered by the people on the other end of the line. Do you not feel the sting and the incredulity when people give you the schlocky excuse that they "skimmed" through your e-mail instead of admitting "I couldn't be bothered to read it"?

Many people have enough trouble with this in their speech, let alone adequately expressing themselves in writing. In speech you can modify your tone, body language, volume or proximity to a person, but print is far less forgiving, especially in the age where people receive hundreds or thousands of messages every day. Your writing has to be compelling.

Over the last several months, I've undergone a huge physical transformation. I've lost nearly 60 pounds and 15 percentage points of body fat, as well as eight inches off my waist. I haven't been this thin and lean since I was twenty-one.

While swiping through my Facebook news feed one day back in 2017, an ad suddenly popped up in front of me, with copy to the effect of: "Are You Tired of Going to the Gym 5-6 Nights a Week and Getting No Results?"

You can bet your bottom dollar I took a second look. First of all, how did they know that I was going to the gym 5-6 nights a week and just adding more fat to my already chubby face and stomach? How would anyone besides my friends know that? And who was this character, Vince Del Monte, advertising on Facebook as if he were reading my mind?

Well, you can't discount Facebook's incredible targeting abilities. Their micro-targeting reaches people that radio and television account executives can only dream of and for a fraction of the cost to the merchant. All that, however, was secondary to the fact that Vince's ad copy seemed to have a camera trained on me; he knew exactly what to say to get my attention. Only three minutes later, he was several dollars richer.

Capital One seems to have observed this because just a few nights before writing this chapter, my wife and I discussed getting a new credit card for my business to keep better track of my expenses and earn cash-back rewards. I didn't post anything about our conversation, but I am profiled on Facebook as a businessman and a marketer, the kind of risk that credit card companies generally love. (If they knew, however, that I'm the type who pays his entire bill in full, they probably wouldn't like me as much).

At any rate, Capital One showed up in my news feed the day after Shannon and I discussed getting the Capital One Business Rewards card. Fancy that! Unlike credit card applications in the past, I experienced the best application process ever. It took me all of one minute to complete the form and submit my information, and I got approved on the spot!

All this is to say that effective communicators in business are making very good use of our self-disclosing proclivities and making it that much more difficult to resist purchasing their products and services. Because we are all addicted to Facebook, LinkedIn, Twitter, InstaGram, and the like, they are reaching us primarily through video, imagery, and well-written words.

The good news, as with public speaking, is that it doesn't take an English degree or the poetic brilliance of William Shakespeare to write in an evocative and engaging manner. You will need to know a few Shakespearean principles, though, and I would be willing to bet money that the Bard knew what I'm about to teach you, even if he himself couldn't articulate it.

Know Your Audience

I observe it over and over - in a networking group, people are thoughtful and careful with what they say or don't say. They can read my body language, they know certain things about me, they discern my personality with great degrees of emotional intelligence, and they choose their words accordingly. I do likewise; I am looser with my jokes and banter among strictly male companions at my cigar/poker game and much more innocent and artful in my play with mixed groups.

For some reason, when it comes to writing e-mail, about 90 percent of people drop all of their tact and intuition. They seem to take no thought regarding how their messages will be interpreted.

By this, I don't mean they all turn into rude jerks; they just suddenly lose all of the firepower they have in person because they reduce their message to plain, bloodless English words. Although writing blandly is *certainly* better than taking the risk of writing something someone would eventually use in a lawsuit, I think we diminish ourselves when we keep to basics.

People become lazy when they address one or more others with a pen or keyboard. Is it because we're communicating into a screen or piece of paper, that the humanity on the receiving end gets obscured? I don't know.

In thinking about this part of the book, I found myself considering some rather hostile e-mails I've received from employers and colleagues in the insurance business over the years. I always want to draw on where I made mistakes, as a means of passing my knowledge on to you. In all of the scenarios I can think of, what failed me was poor written communication. I didn't apply the communication rules I already knew.

In my first insurance job, for example, I worked for a very demanding employer. Part of my job requirement was working every other Saturday from 9:00 to 1:00 to try and set a few extra appointments and close a few more sales.

Even though he wasn't in the office, the agent would send me e-mails to check on my progress. I never felt that I could offer him a satisfactory explanation, so I would reply "Ok" to most of his messages, signaling compliance with his demands but not providing details.

After a few times of doing this, my troubles compounded. He became upset that I was simply replying "Ok." Frustrated and disappointed, I began to keep a scratch notepad by my desk to record my call volume with tick marks. The next time he wrote to check on me, I replied: "50 phone calls, 10 connections, seven rejections, two possibles and one appointment set." This usually diffused him and resulted in a reply to the effect of "Keep at it, you'll find something eventually."

Most people to whom I've told this story side with me automatically, resenting such a level of micro-management. I use the story to illustrate how I failed to employ something I already knew from being a Communications major - "Know your audience."

In this case, my "audience" was my employer. He was a highly critical and easily provoked audience, one I should have known would want concrete details and numbers to satisfy his itch for signs of progress. I *especially* should have known that after about two or three months on the job, but the story I tell happened much later, closer to being on the job about eight or nine months. Replying "Ok" was about the last thing I should have done, yet it took about four or five rounds of confrontation on this issue before I finally picked up on the dissonance between us and changed my responses to his queries.

Content is Key

Generally speaking, I find poorly written material reflects one of two shortcomings. Either we showcase a lack of knowledge/familiarity with the content, or we know *too much* about the topic, so that our answers are cryptic, esoteric, and egg-headed. The first reflects intellectual laziness while the other reveals presumed intellectual superiority. Neither one is useful if you're writing to get a response.

My communication professors at Pacific Lutheran University drilled the importance of audience into me relentlessly. "What use is this to your reader?" they'd scoff. "How are you telling them what you said you were going to tell them?"

After one too many rejected papers, I finally caught on: I was writing my thoughts like a *diary* or journal instead of a letter. I just *dictated* my letter instead of crafting it. When we're writing as professionals, we need to remember there is always more than one brain, one heart, and one soul involved. It's our job to transmit in a language they can receive, relate to, and respond to.

You want the audience to respond *positively*. This book is primarily directed at business and marketing writers and I'm assuming none of you are in the business of actively or consciously offending people. If you're in opinion journalism, you can still apply this principle, but in that case your objective is to get people talking, no matter what they end up saying.

However, many readers of both factual and opinionated work have finished consuming a message and thought, "Well, there's a few minutes of my life I can never get back." As a recovering political talk radio junkie, I have listened to some of the most boring, dull, copycat talk shows out there. All of the talk was provocative and opinionated; some of it was as dull as watching paint dry.

Even with perfect spelling and grammar, you can still be a poor writer. There's no use in being a lawyer with knowledge of the letter of the law, but total ignorance of its spirit. It's the same with writing; I would rather work with a bad speller who knows what his audience will read than an excellent speller who doesn't.

When you craft a letter, take a few moments and *think*:

- Who am I addressing? What are their demographics, commonalities?
- How deep are we going, and how deep are they likely to want to go?
- If I was in the audience, what could someone say that would make me remember them? Insight, humor, courage or perhaps empathy? If you're writing to entrepreneurs, you want boldness, vision and optimism. If you're writing to hurt souls, you want kindness, compassion, soothing wisdom and patience.

- What do you want them to feel after they've read the copy? Is a call for action necessary or overbearing?

- What community are you drawing them into and how can they both benefit and contribute to that community?

The next time you find a book, article or other piece of literature you can't put down, remember this: *They are speaking your language.* They thought of you ahead of time and *that* is why you find it so interesting.

CHAPTER NINE

WASTE NOT, WANT NOT

Here's a personal story in violation of my *Fight Club* rule "The first rule of Selling Insurance is … you do *not talk* about Selling Insurance."

If I could get the recording back, I'd pay hundreds of dollars for it. I was maybe five or six months into my first insurance job, around the summer of 2012. It was a very difficult time for me; I kept setting sales appointments, only to lose them to "walk-outs" after about five minutes in our appointment room. Neither the senior sales rep nor the agency owner could be in the room with me the entire time, so there was no way to fully explain to them what was going wrong.

One day, during an informal sales pep talk, I suggested we secretly record my next appointment, strictly for training purposes. We placed a reliable dictating machine on the shelf in the appointment room, where nobody would notice it. As before, the prospect that came to that appointment got up and walked out, leaving me with the same sales number I had before they walked in. After the dust had settled, the agency owner, senior sales rep and I went into the appointment room to listen to the recording.

I was horrified by the amount of "vomiting" I did. I literally spent the first ten minutes in this man's presence talking 90 percent of time. I asked him few questions outside of what was prepared on the meeting agenda, and I assumed *way* too much about what he thought, felt or how he would receive things I said to him. I never ran another sales appointment the same way. From then on, I forced myself to remain quiet and listen at the same 90% rate I'd been talking.

I came to call this practice "wasting words."

Not so long ago, a younger man representing a publication aimed at the Joint Base Lewis-McChord military audience came to my office and wasted words. I ended up using the occasion to mentor him. It took him fifteen minutes to get his sales shtick off his chest and onto me before he stopped to ask if I was interested. I wanted to say something negative, to try and dissuade him of wasting his time selling print ads. My objection would have been a sweeping generalization; it simply isn't true that *all* print advertising is a waste of time.

Instead, I bluntly told him, "I'm not really targeting military personnel and their families."

"Oh," he said, and sank back a little into his chair.

"Let me tell you a few things I know," I began, reading the disappointment on his face. "Any insurance agent you succeed in selling to in this town has no idea how much of a grip USAA's brand has on the military, and how much money they are about to waste. So you'll be very lucky to pull it off. If I were you, I wouldn't spend another second marketing to insurance agents. You'll end up with jaded, unhappy clients, because you're doing them a disservice and demanding they pay for it.

"Second, you need to know there are businesses here in Olympia and back up in your neck of the woods (Tacoma) whose entire business is marketing to the military." I rattled off about three or four people I knew who fit that profile. He hadn't heard of a single one, but he eagerly wrote them down on a sheet of paper I provided for him.

"Third," I continued, "if you want to sell in Olympia, you need to begin networking. Forget about making the sale. Forget about the quick buck. You're going to have to embed yourself in organizations that work with the military down here. I belong to one and know of several others, but there's no hard/fast sales cycle down here."

The young man thanked me profusely for my advice. He eagerly took copies of the business cards I provided. My colleague, who overheard the conversation, walked in to say how she observed that he seemed brand-new and inexperienced with sales.

I wish that every time I'd done something like this, someone had taken me aside and told me what I was doing wrong, but who knows whether I'd have listened? That too could have been a waste of words.

Often good communication is as much about what you *don't* say as what you *do*. Believe it or not, "silence in print" can carry the same weight as silence in speech. Why do you think we have any discussion today over social issues and the Constitution, or whether God frowns on smoking tobacco products? *Because the texts are silent on the subject.* The authors did not feel the need to micro-manage or dictate to us every little detail. They respected their audiences enough to trust them with the decision. This move proved useful in keeping audiences coming back – which is what any good writer wants.

Interactive news and blog websites and social media have taken traditional media to the cleaners because *their audience can respond.* The beauty of modern marketing communication is that you don't <u>need</u> to waste words. If you can provoke a response, the audience will fill in the blank space.

Although you might ask yourself if you really want an open comments section on your website, audiences are engaging with products and ideas in those kinds of spaces. They're not reading the paper, they're not watching TV news, and they're not listening to the radio. They are keeping each other informed on the latest trends, product failures, and best resources available for their unique needs.

So as you write business copy of any kind, from emails to website content to product descriptions, you need to examine what you write and ask yourself if it's better left unwritten, for reasons that will become clearer in the next chapter.

CHAPTER TEN

THEATER OF THE MIND

Picture a theater. It could be the Sydney Opera House or it could be a Greek amphitheater - it doesn't matter. I want you to think of bright lights on a stage, where columns adorn either side and curtains conceal the backstage crew. We're suddenly amid a busy technical rehearsal, where thespians shuffle and tech workers make one adjustment upon another.

The audience seats are empty save for the directors seated at a table near the front row, rather like how the judges sit on the TV show *America's Got Talent*. There are just two people present, the director with one of his assistants. They hastily review a portion of the script about to be rehearsed, checking for changes in lighting, sound, and visual effects.

There are several whispered conversations backstage about the many subtleties that go into an effective and compelling performance. The main actress, who has ten minutes' lead time before she actually goes onstage, is fighting off a sense of urgency as she sits through the makeup artist's finishing touches.

A few steps away from her, the technical director hisses at his crew, who incorrectly positioned the top lighting two feet behind where the pool of light is supposed to land during the lead actor's soliloquy scene. His order sends them scurrying like ants up ladders and across 2x10 tightropes on their hands and knees to get the lights aimed right.

Meanwhile, an ensemble cast of dancers and singers fidgets nervously backstage. They are clad in leotards and flexible mesh outfits, in order to execute their complex dance steps while belting chorus lines to reinforce the musical interpretation the actors bring to the audience. Some are dialed in and focused while others' attention spans are challenged. Their eyes dart around quickly, from the backstage technical booth to the wings of the theater, where crewmembers and actors shuffle past one another to access green rooms, lighting closets, and other hidden pathways of the catacombs that form a theater.

All of this takes place within seconds, and no sooner do they have the top light fixed and the lead actress' make-up finally applied than the director's commanding voice sails out from the audience to everyone backstage: "Okay, let's run Act Two, Scene Two!"

I used this description to give examples of what you can learn to do in print. Some of you were struck by my use of vocabulary and theater terminology, some by how descriptive I was, and others by how the story built to a little crescendo when the director suddenly called out and stopped all of the action.

You also could have been captured by all three categories or by two. Others perhaps connected to just one and some didn't get it at all. Everyone has some picture in their mind, and that's because we shut off our built-in surveillance cameras and let the central processing system of our brains create the imagery.

The writer in business who can employ detailed description and scenic tension in text has a tremendous opportunity to create strong internal bonds with the reader. If you can successfully tap into their imagination, your business copy can have a profound effect on people and prompt them to do all sorts of things.

You'll know if your copy is effective when people begin to say things like "You have a way of phrasing things so that I can understand," or "I like how you wrote that part; it really made me think."

PART THREE

THE AMBASSADOR

Chapter Eleven

Become The Emblem

Moving with confidence as you do things like networking or writing doesn't come as naturally to many people as it now does for me. I became involved in local Miss America pageants largely because I am so blatantly unafraid of meeting people and making friends. I simply opened my mouth about how I love public speaking, and the next thing you know, I'm standing there in a tuxedo looking like James Bond surrounded by youth and beauty.

People ask, "Where do you get your confidence from?" It's a good question, because I'm not into giving glib answers like "Just believe in yourself" or "Pretend everyone in the audience forgot to wear pants."

The Basics

The Ambassador cannot be a fly on the wall. I learned what I know about being the face of an organization by bothering to show up, and consistently. I joined boards, community associations, and networking groups. I went wherever I was invited, and then some.

There was a time when being "everywhere" was a feat of achievement, but in the age of social media, I've found it isn't nearly so difficult.

One effective method I discovered early on is attending trade shows and community events. Attendance requires some extra hours and can be fruitless if you don't have a strategy to execute. In my coaching programs, we help the community and interpersonal marketer understand the basic "science" of effectively representing their businesses at events. If you follow those steps, you can generate leads and make meaningful connections while you're at it.

In my earliest days at Liberty Mutual, I drove all the way from Olympia to the small agricultural towns of Mossyrock and Morton for some of my first events and gained some of my earliest clients and made some valuable connections. I've never forgotten this, because the people of those towns weren't accustomed to visits from a Liberty Mutual agent. It was rather like we were just opening up new business territory in a state where we'd previously not sold.

In the late summer of 2013, I hosted a table at the Southwest Washington Fair in Centralia. I gathered over 100 leads and had a huge sales month. That event alone set me on the path of scheduling 1-2 events every quarter, hoping to replicate my success.

Over time, I noticed that some events we did turned up hundreds of useless leads, while others turned up only a handful of leads but some very good connections. In the third year I attended the Southwest Washington Fair, I didn't really want people filling out pieces of paper for me to call. I wanted to meet people and drip-market to them over social media. I reaped one large client in 2015, with as much premium as I got from the 10 or 15 clients I wrote from 2013.

From these results, I determined that you will want to have clarity of path before each event. It's important to define why you're paying to sponsor the event. If it's for leads, you need to be a good cold-caller because few of the people who fill out your information slips will remember you, and even fewer will want to talk to you.

If you're there to meet people, however, the object of the game is to make the experience of stopping at your table as interesting as possible. The longer passers-by linger at your table, the more opportunity you have to talk to them. In October 2013 I hosted a table at an event called "Pampering Military Spouses." Looking back on it, I would have made the agenda about meeting people rather than getting leads, because I got 147 leads and not a single sale. I had a line out the door at my table, however, because I partnered with a local masseuse and agreed to cover the cost in exchange for her providing free 10-minute massages to the 99.9% female audience. It would have been a great chance to socialize and get acquainted with some of those spouses, possibly leading to some other connections on Joint Base Lewis-McChord. Instead I went home in ignorant bliss because I had a stack of leads. I didn't know that none of them would pan out.

To be fair to those military spouses, several of them were kind enough to give me a shot at quoting their insurance. But I was fishing in the wrong pool; I simply couldn't offer the price, mobility or pre-existing satisfaction they had with USAA and GEICO.

Nowadays, I develop very clear stipulations at events where I agree to participate:

- There must be an agenda on my part – either branding, lead generation or both
- There must be a way for all event traffic to be directed to my table. The event must hold a raffle or some other method of getting as many attendees as possible to stop by my table at least once.
- There must be an intriguing and attention-getting activity at my table to hold their interest.
- There must be "skin in the game." If you don't want to fill out your name and contact info, that's fine - but I don't give away swag to any adult of sound mind and body who refuses.

Swagger, Justified or Not

If I were to put it into words, I'd say confidence comes from several directions.

By Divine Providence, I assert, I have been through one experience after another of living lengthy periods in close quarters with men older, wiser, and far more committed than I was at the time. Like any influence in excessive amounts, their relational styles simply became a big part of my relational style. I became more assertive, less afraid to ask for what I want, and much likelier to assume responsibility and provide leadership if no one else did.

Between the ages of 20 and 21, I lived rent-free in a beachfront apartment in Santa Monica with a quadriplegic multimillionaire. He'd made a fortune in sales, seminars, and real estate in his native Texas, and retired at age 39 to pursue acting in Southern California. I spent a year living as his assistant, mainly performing physical tasks he could not perform himself. I benefited far more from being under his tutelage, though, than he ever did from my ordinary muscular strength.

In the military, I served under two cadres of noncommissioned officers with tremendous work ethics and dedication to the mission. They made clear to me, first by excluding me when I performed poorly and then by including me when I caught onto their agenda, that my maturity had a long way to go and wasn't going to come cheap. This lesson was especially hard to avoid during a total of 26 months in combat on Operation Iraqi Freedom;

there's no way such a lesson wouldn't influence a young and impressionable man.

Another huge component of confidence goes back to the rule of not saying too much; it is better to be a fool and be silent than to open your mouth and remove all doubt. In my time, in the military especially, I observed the effect of "pecking order." If you're brand-new in your platoon, for example, you keep almost dead silent, and let the soldiers and officers who have been around for a while to do the talking. Then you gradually pipe up here and there, and eventually you're accepted and free to talk at will.

After leaving military service, I took what I learned there into civilian networking situations. I discovered that my personality type is considered extremely presumptuous if I simply walk into a meeting, where I am a complete stranger, and expected to be welcomed in. I made it a policy, after a while, to not attend a function to which I hadn't been invited by anyone.

I used to go to activities like the Thurston County Volunteer Legal Services Breakfast, an assembly of most of the city's legal professionals, or the Thurston-Mason County Dental Society's annual golf tournament. Although I did make some friends there, it was clear they perceived that I was primarily interested in selling insurance. We've already been over Rule #1 about Selling Insurance.

This led to a new set of discoveries, because often I found events or functions I *wanted* to be a part of, but couldn't think of any compelling reason *why* I should be there. The last thing you want, as an insurance salesman, is for the other people attending the event to think, "Oh boy, another insurance salesman wanting my money."

These days, when I get invited to something, it is rarely just because someone was kind enough to extend the invitation. Usually it is the result of reciprocation, where I have invested time, money or energy into someone, or offered to help them in return. At some of my first speaking engagements, for example, I enlisted the help of a good friend, who excels at acquiring data and payments, to run the logistics of my table for pre-selling books and adding people to my e-mail list. In exchange, I offered to donate a portion of my book sales to her daughter's cheerleading booster club.

That kind of thinking ahead led to reciprocation; my friend started inviting me to other gatherings where she knew people I didn't - and when the topic of what I do for a living comes up, opportunities, large and small, were created.

Embrace the Prep

The third leg of this stool is a big one: *preparation*.

You may remember, or at least have heard of, President Ronald Reagan. There are many things about him that most people can trace to his memory like "Tear down this wall," his famous line to Mikhail Gorbachev; his speech after the space shuttle Challenger disaster; or his quip during the 1984 debate promising not to hold his opponent's youth and inexperience against him.

Not much is said, though, about Reagan's skill at *preparation*. If people understood how *prepared* Reagan was, they'd have better insight into why he was so successful at connecting with the American people. His two consecutive landslide elections should remove all doubt, especially, his re-election where he won 49 states and 58% of the popular vote.

To understand President Reagan, you have to consider his career experience as a radio sports announcer, a B-movie actor, a Hollywood anti-communist, a speaker/trainer for General Electric, and, of course, governor of California. Reagan had spent a lifetime in front of audiences of all kinds, speaking and persuading. And that means he spent even more time *rehearsing*.

Paul Kengor's book *The Crusader: Ronald Reagan and the Fall of Communism* revealed Reagan's dogged determination. The future US president rose through the ranks in Hollywood, and Reagan frequently found himself in the middle of the fray between the unions that came to dominate the motion picture industry – chief among them, the Screen Actors Guild and the American Federation of Television and Radio Artists.

It was during their disputes that Reagan developed a distaste for revolutionary politics. He felt that the communist element in Hollywood was abusing the Democratic Party's roots of supporting workers' rights, a cause he believed in. He was also physically present for so many of these debates that he began to notice patterns.

The people who shouted the loudest during union meetings, according to Reagan, always sat in the same seats in the house. They formed a "diamond" formation – some at the front, some in the middle on either end, and some at the back. Reagan began to notice that they were often the same people each time or a rotation of familiar faces.

It was from this that Reagan developed his staunch anti-communism view, because he learned that the agitators were often members of the Communist Party or an aligned socialist group. Their presence and dominance at these meetings was no accident, nor was it simply coincidence. He took to heart the importance of preparation in meeting their vociferous members head-on.

From those days in the early 1940s, Reagan became a one-man battalion against the communists, fighting them at every turn. He also used his skills as an actor to become a very persuasive and passionate orator, delivering the famous speech "A Time For Choosing" on behalf of Barry Goldwater in the 1964 presidential election.

As he entered politics, Reagan also saw that humor and wit made fantastic tools for retaliating against his opponents, and he began scripting comedic observations into his speeches. By the time he was elected president in 1980, he was already well known for simplifying complicated arguments into one-liners: "How come when we spend our money, it's inflationary, but when the government spends our money, it isn't?" he quipped on the *Johnny Carson Show* in 1978.

Throughout his presidency, in campaigns and in executing the office, Reagan was known to spend hours rehearsing his jokes and speeches. He became "The Great Communicator" because he was *prepared*. He had been forged in ideological struggle, in competition for the hearts and minds of American voters, and in the simple act of carrying index cards with his jokes and one-liners so that he could master their delivery.

Shyness, anxiety, or just plain preference of being solitary may weaken your confidence, but there is *nothing* stopping you from preparing to move with confidence in the marketplace.

So what do we do?

In networking I like to interact with a humor that is both self-promoting and self-deprecating at the same time, which gives people both a feeling of confidence and something to laugh at. Given half the chance, I will jump at a chance to be on the microphone because I know how to talk.

Here's the secret: *I didn't make this up on my own.*

I learned to have confidence in public by watching how people do things well, and watching how other people do things poorly.

For instance, at my monthly poker and cigar night, I learned how to make myself entertaining and endearing by watching Raul Julia play Gomez Addams in *The Addams Family*. I greet everyone with some kind of modifier – usually the words "old man" after their name, with a lit cigar in my mouth and a big firm handshake with a clap on the back. It's always well received, because it matches with my personality.

When I go back to my office, I bag that routine and take up the subtly humorous demeanor of a former colleague of mine. I say funny lines in a serious-sounding voice, almost like Leslie Nielsen would say them in movies like *Airplane!* or the *Naked Gun* trilogy.

When I go to a networking group in town, I rely on quick wit and one-liners. An associate rose to compliment me for taking care of their client, and had to prompt me to stand up to receive it. I rose and said, unabashedly, "I would NEVER attempt to make the conversation about *myself*." Everyone laughed along, knowing that I was promoting myself and laughing at myself at the same time. This is one

I actually modified from a sincere statement made by a mentor with a similar brand of sarcasm and exaggeration.

On Fridays, I usually join another group of businessmen at a local restaurant for lunch and within this group I'm known as the bodybuilder. The restaurant owner and I are both big fans of Arnold Schwarzenegger, so I frequently say things like "It's not a tu-mah!"

Preparation takes practice, and you have to know when to use which kind of energy … but when you do, it changes how people perceive you.

The Good, the Bad, the Ugly

Lastly, I would like to speak in appreciation of the value of plain old sincerity. One of the things I really like about living in the age we do is that it is a statement of strength to confess to and be vulnerable about our weaknesses.

If you can walk onto a stage in front of an audience of any size and take the risk of exposing mistakes or poor decisions you've made, you won't need a pithy remark or comeback to secure bonds with your audience. As a recovering addict, I have made several friends who are also recovering from addiction. Without exception, we have found strength in great supply when we can readily confess to our compulsions and inappropriate behaviors.

Perhaps riding the strength of this phenomenon, there is even a scene in the film *Star Wars: The Last Jedi* that specifically states this. Luke Skywalker, troubled by his failures as a Jedi Master, gets a special visit from Yoda, who reminds him to pass on what he has learned in an effective way. We have to teach about legends and triumphs and wisdom, of course; we also have to share about our mistakes, our failures and the dark places it took us.

People are drawn to vulnerability. There are as few people who can relate to being perfect on this planet as there are billions of beings who can relate to making mistakes and failing. That's why I proclaim that what you have learned here was paid for in regret, sorrow, ostracism and looking like a dope. We intellectually understand the saying, "To err is human." It's a pity it's taken us so long to understand that revealing our humanity gives us such an advantage with our fellow human beings. I have yet to see honesty fail, as you've probably noticed, since it's a recurring theme in this book.

CONCLUSION

One thing I've learned about the business of information and knowledge is that it's impossible to contain everything we need to know in one volume. If the Bible itself is not comprehensive, I do not feel bad that I haven't answered *every* question that could come up in response to what is written.

I do, however, have more answers, ideas and tools than you currently hold in your hands. Visit my website, www.thepaulsedwards.com, to learn about workshops, masterminds and coaching programs.

You'll find me easily on Facebook, InstaGram, LinkedIn and Twitter under "@thepaulsedwards."

E-mails are welcomed and appreciated. I receive a lot of them and try to answer as many as I can. Send me your feedback at edsvoices@yahoo.com. Hate mail and negative, snarky responses should be directed to myjunkmail@gmail.com where they will promptly be ignored and discarded.

It is my sincere hope that you are empowered and encouraged by the examples and stories I've set forth in this book. Marketing methods change, but the laws and the principles of the universe remain steadfast. I believe deeply that what I teach here is derived from the latter, which means that when the methods of the early 21st Century become obsolete, this book will still be relevant to the generations that succeed mine.

But that itself will be a subject for revision, and could be my next, best mistake to write about.

ACKNOWLEDGMENTS

This book owes so much to the value principle of its content that I don't know I can fully describe it. Just as my business and influence have grown from the strengths of many, so has the inspiration and fulfillment of this small portion of my dream.

I am indebted to some of my strongest local, national and international marketing allies and friends. These people, each in small but noticeable ways, paved the broken road for this book to reach editing and printing. Thank you to my friend Alan Shimamoto for planting the seed long ago, suggesting I begin presenting and speaking on the subject – and for continued interest and insight as we moved the ball down the field (#GoBroncos).

Thank you to Sara Younger, who became a "protégé" of sorts and showed me just how much motivated people can "pass you up" when you teach them what they want to know. Sara also deserves a mountain of credit for the connections she provided through Saturn Barter to make this project happen at a fraction of the cost it would normally incur.

Thank you to Dave Culbreath, my ally in Christ and a pure blessing of relief in the area of website design and construction.

Thank you to my "air war" mentors from afar – Vince Del Monte, Russell Brunson, Bedros Keuilian and Craig Ballantyne.

No good literary work enters the marketplace without a gifted and vigilant editor. I am profoundly grateful for Rebecca Mabanglo-Mayor's keen eye and attention to detail, and it's always reassured me that we both learned professional communication from the same content-obsessed professors at PLU.

My wife, Shannon Edwards, and my sons Grant and Chase Edwards – I owe so much of the success of this work to you and the constant spiritual nourishment of a loyal and loving family. This book got completed in the margins of life and I appreciate your support and understanding as I worked to make it a reality.

And God Almighty, Jesus Christ, the King of Kings – I beseech and welcome your blessing, your contribution and the origins of this content directly from your sovereign hand. I know that this book, at its core, is a mere reflection of principles and laws you've long since established in the universe, but which I have only discovered in the last few years. May your name be glorified and your Kingdom further established by its success and influence. Thank you for the gifts and talents you gave me; my prayer is that I've used them well.

Yours,
Paul

www.ingramcontent.com/pod-product-compliance
Lightning Source LLC
Chambersburg PA
CBHW061611220326
41598CB00024BC/3550